LOIRE VA

TRAVEL GUIDE

2025

Art and History in the Loire Valley: Museums, Galleries, and Cultural Landmarks.

BY

ZERA CANTRELL

Copyright © 2024 ZERA CANTRELL.

All Rights Reserved.

Table of Contents

Disclaimer 5

Introduction 7

    Why Visit the Loire Valley? 9

    Quick Facts and Travel Tips 12

Chapter 1: Exploring the Châteaux 17

    Château de Chambord: The Epitome of French Renaissance 17

    Château de Chenonceau: The Ladies' Castle 20

    Château de Villandry: Gardens of Enchantment ... 24

    Château d'Amboise: Royal Residence and Da Vinci's Last Home 27

Chapter 2: Insider Tips for Visiting Multiple Châteaux 31

    Historic Towns and Villages 31

    Tours: A Blend of Old and New 33

    Blois: Royal History and Architectural Marvels ... 37

    Saumur: The Home of Cadre Noir and Sparkling Wines . 40

    Orléans: Joan of Arc's Legacy 43

    Best Villages to Experience Traditional Loire Valley Life 46

Chapter 3: Wine and Gastronomy 51

The Vineyards of the Loire: A Guide to Wine Regions......51

Wine Tasting Tours: Where and How..............................54

Local Cuisine: Must-Try Dishes and Where to Find Them
....58

Farmers' Markets: Fresh Produce and Artisan Goods......61

Cooking Classes: Learn to Cook Like a Local...................64

Chapter 4: Outdoor Adventures..69

Cycling the Loire à Vélo: The Ultimate Biking Experience
....69

Walking and Hiking Trails: Discover Nature's Beauty.....72

Hot Air Balloon Rides: A Bird's Eye View of the Valley....75

River Activities: Kayaking and Canoeing on the Loire......77

Chapter 5: Arts and Culture 81

Museums and Galleries: Art and History.........................81

Festivals and Events: Celebrating Local Traditions 84

Music and Performing Arts: The Best Venues and
Performances 87

Chapter 6: Family-Friendly Activities....................................91

Kid-Friendly Châteaux: Fun for the Whole Family...........91

Parks and Playgrounds: Let the Little Ones Run Wild.....94

storied connection to Joan of Arc, provide unique insights into the region's diverse character.

Indulge in the region's culinary treasures with our guide to the best local wines and dishes, and learn where to find the freshest produce at bustling farmers' markets. For those seeking adventure, cycling the Loire à Vélo, hiking scenic trails, or even taking a hot air balloon ride will reveal the valley's natural splendor from new heights.

Whether you are a history buff, a wine enthusiast, a nature lover, or a family seeking fun, this guide is designed to enrich your journey with practical tips, local secrets, and inspiring stories. As you explore the Loire Valley, may you be captivated by its charm and grace, and carry home memories that will linger long after your visit.

So, turn the page and let the magic of the Loire Valley unfold before you. Your adventure begins here.

Why Visit the Loire Valley?

Châteaux Extravaganza

The Loire Valley is synonymous with its magnificent châteaux, each with its own unique story and architectural style. Château de Chambord (41250 Chambord, France) is a masterpiece of Renaissance architecture. Its intricate façade and the double-helix staircase, designed by Leonardo da Vinci, are a testament to its grandeur. A visit here is like stepping back into a fairy tale, with expansive grounds perfect for leisurely strolls and picnic spots.

A short drive away is the Château de Chenonceau (37150 Chenonceaux, France), often called the "Ladies' Castle" due to the influential women who shaped its history. The château stretches gracefully over the Cher River, and its gardens, especially the Diane de Poitiers and Catherine de Medici gardens, are spectacular. The blend of history and natural beauty here is simply enchanting.

Don't miss the Château de Villandry (37510 Villandry, France), renowned for its elaborate Renaissance gardens. The symmetry and design of the gardens are a gardener's dream, offering a serene escape and stunning photo opportunities.

Culinary and Viticultural Riches

The Loire Valley's culinary scene is equally impressive. The region is celebrated for its wines, particularly its crisp whites and exquisite rosés. Domaine de la Taille aux Loups (37110 Montlouis-sur-Loire, France) is a must-visit for wine enthusiasts. The estate's natural, organic practices and the unique flavors of their wines offer a true taste of the valley.

For a quintessential Loire Valley dining experience, head to La Maison d'à Côté (23 Rue des Vinaigriers, 41350 Montlivault, France). The restaurant, known for its inventive approach to traditional French cuisine, features locally sourced ingredients and seasonal dishes that showcase the best of the region's produce.

Picturesque Villages and Towns

Exploring the charming towns and villages of the Loire Valley is a highlight of any visit. Tours (37000 Tours, France), the region's largest city, offers a vibrant atmosphere with its bustling markets and historic buildings. The Place Plumereau is particularly noteworthy, with its medieval architecture and lively cafes. The weekly market here is perfect for sampling local cheeses, pastries, and other delicacies.

Amboise (37400 Amboise, France), a town with strong royal connections, is home to the Château d'Amboise, where Leonardo da Vinci spent his final years. The town's narrow streets and quaint shops are delightful to explore, and the local Marché d'Amboise provides a great opportunity to experience regional flavors.

In Saumur (49400 Saumur, France), you'll find the famous Cadre Noir equestrian school and a range of excellent sparkling wines. The Musée des Beaux-Arts here offers a diverse art collection, and the surrounding vineyards are ideal for a leisurely afternoon tasting.

Natural Beauty and Outdoor Activities

The Loire Valley's natural landscapes are as captivating as its historical sites. The Loire à Vélo cycling route offers scenic rides through vineyards, orchards, and along the river, providing a fantastic way to experience the region's beauty. For a more leisurely outdoor experience, the Parc Floral de la Source (Boulevard Charles de Gaulle, 45000 Orléans, France) in Orléans features beautifully landscaped gardens and tranquil paths.

Quick Facts and Travel Tips

Essential Facts

Location: The Loire Valley stretches along the Loire River in central France, covering parts of the Centre-Val de Loire and Pays de la Loire regions.

Best Time to Visit: The ideal times to visit are spring (April to June) and autumn (September to October). During these periods, the weather is pleasant, and the crowds are smaller. Summer is also a popular time, but expect more tourists and higher temperatures.

Language: French is the official language. While English is commonly spoken in tourist areas, learning a few basic French phrases can enhance your experience.

Currency: The currency used is the Euro (€). Credit and debit cards are widely accepted, but it's useful to carry some cash for small purchases and in rural areas.

Time Zone: Central European Time (CET), which is GMT+1. Daylight Saving Time (CEST) is observed from late March to late October.

Climate: The Loire Valley enjoys a temperate climate with warm summers and mild winters. Expect average summer temperatures between 20°C and 25°C (68°F to 77°F) and cooler winter temperatures around 5°C to 10°C (41°F to 50°F).

Travel Tips

Getting There:

By Train: The TGV (high-speed train) connects Paris to Tours, a major gateway to the Loire Valley. The journey takes about 1.5 hours. From Tours, you can use regional trains or car rentals to explore other parts of the valley.

By Car: Renting a car is highly recommended for flexibility. The drive from Paris to the Loire Valley takes about 2.5 hours. Major rental agencies operate at Paris Charles de Gaulle Airport and in central Paris.

By Plane: The nearest major airport is Tours Val de Loire Airport (TUF), offering flights from Paris and other French cities. Alternatively, you can fly into Nantes Atlantique Airport (NTE) or Paris Orly Airport (ORY) and drive to the valley.

Transportation Within the Valley:

Car Rental: Essential for exploring châteaux and rural areas. Rental locations are available in Tours, Blois, and Saumur.

Biking: The Loire à Vélo cycle route offers a scenic way to explore the region. Bike rentals are available in major towns like Tours and Amboise.

Public Transport: Buses connect major towns, but services can be infrequent. For a more immersive experience, consider guided tours that include transportation.

Accommodation:

Luxury: Château de Noizay, 37310 Noizay. A splendid 16th-century château with luxurious rooms and gardens.

Mid-Range: Hôtel de l'Univers, 33 Rue du Général de Gaulle, 37000 Tours. Comfortable rooms with modern amenities in the heart of Tours.

Budget: Ibis Styles Blois Centre, 1-8 Rue Louise Michel, 41000 Blois. Affordable and convenient, with easy access to Blois' attractions.

Dining:

Gastronomy: Try La Maison des Bois, 6 Place de la République, 37500 Chinon, for fine dining with a focus on local ingredients.

Casual: L'Auberge du Bon Laboureur, 1 Rue du Docteur Bretonneau, 37400 Amboise. A charming bistro offering traditional Loire Valley cuisine.

Local Specialties: Sample goat cheese from local farms and the region's famous wines, including Vouvray and Sancerre.

Local Customs:

Dining Etiquette: Meals are often leisurely. It's customary to wait for the host to start before eating.

Tipping: Service is usually included in your bill, but a small additional tip for exceptional service is appreciated.

Health and Safety:

Health: Ensure you have comprehensive travel insurance. The region is generally safe, but standard precautions apply.

Emergency Services: Dial 112 for emergencies. The local medical facilities are well-equipped and accessible.

Chapter 1: Exploring the Châteaux

Château de Chambord: The Epitome of French Renaissance

Address: Château de Chambord, 41250 Chambord, France

Phone: +33 2 54 50 40 00

Website: chambord.org

The Château de Chambord stands as a towering symbol of the French Renaissance, a masterpiece of architecture and design that has captivated visitors for centuries. Nestled in the heart of the Loire Valley, this grandiose castle is a must-see for anyone seeking to understand the opulence and artistry of 16th-century France.

Architectural Marvel

Designed by Domenico da Cortona, a Renaissance architect from Italy, Chambord is renowned for its striking symmetry and intricate detailing. The château's design is an ambitious fusion of French medieval and Italian Renaissance styles, marked by its 440 rooms, 282 fireplaces, and 77 staircases. The most iconic feature is the double helix staircase, which allows two people to ascend and descend without ever meeting—an engineering marvel that showcases the inventive spirit of the time. This staircase is not only functional but also serves as a centerpiece of the château's design, symbolizing the grandeur and sophistication of the Renaissance era.

The Royal Connection

Chambord was commissioned by King Francis I, who sought a hunting lodge that would reflect his status and showcase the latest architectural innovations. Though he never spent much time here, the château was designed to impress and to serve as a grand stage for royal hunting parties and state events. The castle's large moat and surrounding parkland (spanning over 13,000 acres) underscore its purpose as a hunting retreat, providing ample space for the king and his court to pursue game.

The Gardens and Grounds

The château's grounds are as impressive as the building itself. The meticulously manicured gardens, designed by the famous landscape architect Jean-Baptiste de La Quintinie, offer a serene contrast to the grandeur of the château. Visitors can explore the vast parklands, which include formal gardens, a beautiful French-style canal, and scenic walking paths. Seasonal events, such as garden tours and outdoor concerts, further enhance the visitor experience, allowing guests to immerse themselves in the château's historical ambiance.

Inside the Château

Stepping inside Chambord is like entering a different era. The interior is a labyrinth of lavishly decorated rooms, each telling a different story of French royalty and Renaissance art. The king's apartments, located on the main floor, feature elaborate tapestries, richly carved wooden paneling, and opulent furniture. The château's numerous salons and galleries are adorned with artworks and period pieces, offering a glimpse into the regal lifestyle of the 16th century.

Visitor Tips

To make the most of your visit to Château de Chambord, consider the following tips:

Arrive Early: The château is a popular destination, especially during peak tourist season. Arriving early can help you avoid the crowds and enjoy a more intimate experience.

Guided Tours: Opt for a guided tour to gain deeper insights into the history and architectural significance of the château.

Audio guides are also available for those who prefer to explore at their own pace.

Photography: While photography is permitted, be mindful of the restrictions in certain areas, such as the historic rooms where flash photography is not allowed.

Dining: There are dining options within the château grounds, including a café and a more formal restaurant. Reservations are recommended for the latter, especially during high season.

Accessibility

The château is accessible to visitors with limited mobility, though some areas may be challenging due to the historic nature of the building. Wheelchair rentals are available, and the staff are generally helpful in accommodating special needs.

Château de Chenonceau: The Ladies' Castle

Historical Background

Château de Chenonceau's history is woven with the lives of several influential women, who each left their mark on its legacy. Originally constructed in the early 16th century by

Thomas Bohier and his wife, Catherine, the château's story truly began to take shape when Catherine's daughter-in-law, Diane de Poitiers, became its primary patron. Diane, a prominent figure in the court of King Henry II, was instrumental in shaping the château's appearance and functionality. Her influence is particularly evident in the elegant gallery that extends over the Cher River—a feature that defines the castle's unique and romantic silhouette.

Following Henry II's death, the château came into the possession of Catherine de' Medici, Henry's widow. Catherine, another formidable woman of her time, further enhanced the castle, transforming it into a luxurious residence with an elaborate garden that still captivates visitors today.

Architectural Highlights

Château de Chenonceau is renowned for its breathtaking architecture. The castle's most striking feature is its long gallery, which spans the Cher River. This Renaissance masterpiece, measuring over 60 meters in length, is adorned with large windows that offer panoramic views of the river and surrounding gardens. The gallery's stunning frescoes and intricate woodwork reflect the opulence of the era and provide a glimpse into the castle's illustrious past.

The château's interiors are equally impressive, with elegantly furnished rooms that showcase period furniture, tapestries, and art. Highlights include the regal King's Room, which once belonged to Henry II, and the Queen's Room, associated with Catherine de' Medici. The rooms are meticulously preserved, offering a fascinating insight into 16th-century French aristocratic life.

Gardens and Grounds

The gardens of Château de Chenonceau are as enchanting as the castle itself. The estate features several distinct gardens, each with its own character. Diane de Poitiers' Garden, with its symmetrical layout and serene atmosphere, contrasts beautifully with Catherine de' Medici's Garden, which is known for its rich floral displays and intricate design. The castle's vast parkland also includes a kitchen garden, where herbs and vegetables are grown using traditional methods.

The castle grounds extend along the Cher River, providing picturesque walking paths and tranquil spots for reflection. The natural beauty of the surrounding landscape complements the castle's grandeur, making it a perfect setting for a leisurely stroll or a relaxing afternoon.

Visitor Information

Address: Château de Chenonceau, 37150 Chenonceaux, France

Opening Hours: The château is typically open daily from 9:00 AM to 6:00 PM, with extended hours during peak seasons. It's advisable to check the official website for current hours and any special closures.

Admission: Tickets cost around €15 for adults, with discounts available for students, seniors, and children. Guided tours and audio guides are available for an additional fee.

How to Get There: Château de Chenonceau is conveniently located approximately 2.5 hours by train from Paris, with the closest major station being Tours. From Tours, you can take a regional train or bus to Chenonceaux. By car, the château is about a 2-hour drive from Paris, with ample parking available.

Tips for Visitors

Arrive Early: To avoid the crowds and fully appreciate the château's beauty, it's best to arrive early in the day.

Dress Comfortably: The castle's extensive grounds and gardens are best explored on foot, so wear comfortable shoes.

Photography: While photography is allowed in the gardens, please note that it is restricted inside the castle.

Château de Villandry: Gardens of Enchantment

Address: Château de Villandry, 37190 Villandry, France

Opening Hours: Typically open daily from 9:00 AM to 6:00 PM, with extended hours in peak season. Check the official website for seasonal variations and special closures.

The Gardens: A Masterpiece of Design

The gardens at Château de Villandry are the highlight of any visit. They were meticulously designed in the early 16th century by Jean Le Breton, a former finance minister for King Francis I, and have been lovingly restored to reflect their original splendor. The gardens are divided into several distinct areas, each with its own theme and character.

The Ornamental Gardens:

The Ornamental Gardens are a marvel of symmetry and color. Here, geometric patterns and vibrant flowerbeds create a striking visual impact. The gardens are arranged in intricate designs, featuring a mix of seasonal flowers that change throughout the year, ensuring that each visit offers something new. The color palette and arrangement are carefully curated to provide a harmonious and visually stunning experience.

The Vegetable Gardens:

In stark contrast to the ornamental gardens, the Vegetable Gardens showcase a more practical but equally impressive design. These gardens demonstrate the Renaissance passion for both beauty and utility, with neatly arranged beds of vegetables and herbs forming geometric patterns. The vegetable gardens not only provide a feast for the eyes but also supply the château's kitchen with fresh produce, bridging the gap between aesthetics and practicality.

The Water Gardens:

The Water Gardens at Villandry offer a serene and tranquil experience. The tranquil pools and reflective surfaces provide a calm escape from the more vibrant areas of the gardens. This section features elegant water features, including fountains and lily ponds, set against lush greenery. The design emphasizes harmony and peace, inviting visitors to relax and reflect.

The Garden of Love:

This area of the garden is dedicated to the theme of love, with each section symbolizing different aspects of romantic affection. The design uses a combination of plants and sculptures to convey messages of love and devotion. It's a romantic spot perfect for a quiet stroll or to simply sit and contemplate the beauty around you.

The Maze:

One of the most enjoyable features for families and those young at heart is the garden maze. This classic labyrinth is designed to challenge and entertain visitors as they navigate through the neatly trimmed hedges. It's an engaging way to explore the gardens and have a bit of fun.

Visiting Tips

Guided Tours: For an enriched experience, consider joining a guided tour. These tours provide historical context and detailed insights into the design and significance of the gardens.

Photography: The gardens offer numerous photo opportunities. Early morning or late afternoon light can be particularly magical, casting soft shadows and highlighting the intricate details of the garden designs.

Accessibility: The gardens are generally accessible, but some areas may be challenging for those with mobility issues due to uneven surfaces.

Nearby Attractions:

Château de Langeais: Located about 20 kilometers from Villandry, this château features a fascinating medieval architecture and history.

Château d'Azay-le-Rideau: Another gem in the Loire Valley, this château is known for its picturesque setting on the Indre River.

Dining Options:

La Table de Villandry: Located near the château, this restaurant offers a delightful selection of regional dishes, ideal for enjoying after a day of exploring the gardens.

Château d'Amboise: Royal Residence and Da Vinci's Last Home

A Brief History

The Château d'Amboise, originally a medieval fortress, was transformed into a grand Renaissance residence by King Charles VIII in the late 15th century. Under the reign of subsequent monarchs, including Louis XII and Francis I, the château evolved into one of the most important royal residences of the period. Its strategic location offered a panoramic view of the Loire Valley and the river below, making it a favored retreat for French royalty.

Exploring the Château

The château's architecture is a fascinating blend of Gothic and Renaissance styles, with its most notable features being the grand staircase and the richly decorated interiors. The main entrance is adorned with an impressive facade, while the interior courtyards reveal elegant arcades and detailed stonework.

The pièce de résistance is undoubtedly the château's spiral staircase, designed by Domenico da Cortona. This exquisite staircase, often referred to as the "Grand Escalier," exemplifies Renaissance design and provides stunning views of the surrounding landscape from its observation platform.

Leonardo da Vinci's Legacy

Leonardo da Vinci's connection to Château d'Amboise adds a layer of historical intrigue. In 1516, Leonardo, then in his early sixties, moved to the château at the invitation of King Francis I. The great artist and polymath spent the last three years of his life here, in a residence known as the "Clos

Lucé," which is situated just a short walk from the main château.

During his time at Amboise, Leonardo worked on various projects and shared his knowledge with the French court. His presence at the château is commemorated with a dedicated exhibition at the Clos Lucé, which showcases some of his original manuscripts, sketches, and models of his inventions. The Clos Lucé is now a museum that beautifully preserves the legacy of da Vinci's final years and is a must-visit for any art and history enthusiast.

Visitor Information

Château d'Amboise

Address: Montée de l'Impérial, 37400 Amboise, France

Opening Hours: Typically open daily from 9:00 AM to 6:00 PM. Hours may vary seasonally, so it's advisable to check the official website before planning your visit.

Admission Fees: Prices vary based on age and season. Adult tickets are around €15, with discounts available for children and groups.

Clos Lucé

Address: 2 Rue du Clos Lucé, 37400 Amboise, France

Opening Hours: Open daily from 9:00 AM to 18:30 PM. Again, check the website for current timings and ticket prices.

Admission Fees: Tickets are approximately €12 for adults, with reduced rates for children and families.

Tips for Visitors

Early Arrival: To avoid the crowds and fully appreciate the château's serene atmosphere, arrive early in the day.

Guided Tours: Consider taking a guided tour to gain deeper insights into the château's history and its royal significance.

Comfortable Footwear: The château's extensive grounds and historical stairs can be uneven, so wear comfortable walking shoes.

Photography: Both the château and Clos Lucé offer fantastic photo opportunities, so don't forget your camera.

Chapter 2: Insider Tips for Visiting Multiple Châteaux

Historic Towns and Villages

Tours: A Blend of Old and New

Begin your journey in Tours, a city that beautifully balances modernity with its medieval heritage. Start at the Cathédrale Saint-Gatien (Place de la Cathédrale, 37000 Tours), a stunning Gothic cathedral with intricate stained glass windows and twin towers. Stroll through the Old Town (Vieux Tours), where narrow cobblestone streets are lined with half-timbered houses and lively cafes. Don't miss the Place Plumereau, often bustling with students and locals enjoying the vibrant atmosphere. The Musée des Beaux-Arts (18 Place François Sicard, 37000 Tours) houses an impressive collection of paintings, sculptures, and decorative arts, making it a cultural highlight of the city.

Blois: Royal History and Architectural Marvels

Next, head to Blois, a town steeped in royal history. The Château de Blois (6 Place du Château, 41000 Blois) is a must-visit, with its fascinating blend of Gothic, Renaissance, and Classical architecture. Each wing tells a different story, from the dramatic assassination of the Duke of Guise to the whimsical decorations of King Louis XII. The town itself is a joy to explore, with winding streets leading to stunning views over the Loire River. The Maison de la Magie (1 Place du Château, 41000 Blois), dedicated to the famous illusionist Robert-Houdin, adds a touch of enchantment to your visit.

Saumur: The Home of Cadre Noir and Sparkling Wines

Saumur, known for its equestrian tradition and sparkling wines, is another gem. The Château de Saumur (49400 Saumur), perched on a hill overlooking the town, offers panoramic views and a deep dive into the region's history. The Cadre Noir (Avenue de l'Ecole Nationale d'Equitation, 49400 Saumur), the prestigious national horse-riding school, offers fascinating tours and mesmerizing equestrian shows. Wine enthusiasts should not miss a visit to the Caves Louis de Grenelle (Rue Marceau, 49400 Saumur), where you can tour the cellars and sample some of the best sparkling wines in the region.

Orléans: Joan of Arc's Legacy

Orléans, forever linked with Joan of Arc, is a city of resilience and beauty. The Cathédrale Sainte-Croix (Place Sainte-Croix, 45000 Orléans), with its towering spires and impressive facade, stands as a testament to the city's storied past. Follow in the footsteps of the Maid of Orléans at the Maison de Jeanne d'Arc (3 Place du Général de Gaulle, 45000 Orléans), a museum dedicated to her life and legacy. The Hôtel Groslot (Place de l'Étape, 45000 Orléans), a Renaissance mansion, offers a glimpse into the opulent life of the city's past inhabitants.

Best Villages to Experience Traditional Loire Valley Life

For a more intimate experience, visit some of the region's enchanting villages. Candes-Saint-Martin, located at the confluence of the Loire and Vienne rivers, is a picture-perfect spot with its white tufa stone houses and scenic river views. Montsoreau, featured in Alexandre Dumas' novel "La Dame de Montsoreau," boasts a charming château and beautiful riverside paths. Another gem is Crissay-sur-Manse, often listed among the most beautiful villages in France, with its medieval architecture and tranquil ambiance.

Tours: A Blend of Old and New

Exploring the Historic Heart of Tours

Begin your journey in the historic heart of Tours, known as Vieux Tours. The narrow cobblestone streets, half-timbered houses, and charming squares transport you back in time. Start at Place Plumereau, a picturesque square surrounded by medieval buildings with vibrant café terraces. Here, you can enjoy a leisurely coffee at Le Bartok (15 Place Plumereau, 37000 Tours) and watch the world go by.

A short walk from Place Plumereau brings you to the impressive Cathédrale Saint-Gatien (5 Place de la Cathédrale, 37000 Tours). This Gothic masterpiece, with its stunning stained glass windows and soaring towers, is a testament to the city's rich religious history. Don't miss the opportunity to explore the cathedral's interior, where intricate details and a serene atmosphere await.

Adjacent to the cathedral is the Musée des Beaux-Arts de Tours (18 Place François Sicard, 37000 Tours), housed in the former bishop's palace. This museum boasts an impressive collection of paintings, sculptures, and decorative arts spanning from the Renaissance to the modern era. Highlights include works by Rubens, Rembrandt, and Delacroix.

The Vibrant Modern Side of Tours

Tours is not just about history; it's a vibrant city that embraces modernity. Head to Rue Nationale, the city's main shopping street, where a mix of high-end boutiques, department stores, and charming shops line the boulevard. For a unique shopping experience, visit Les Halles de Tours (Place Gaston Pailhou, 37000 Tours), a bustling covered market where you can find fresh produce, local cheeses, and gourmet delights.

For a taste of contemporary art, visit the CCC OD - Centre de Création Contemporaine Olivier Debré (Jardin François 1er, 37000 Tours). This modern art center hosts rotating exhibitions featuring works by both established and emerging artists. The sleek, minimalist architecture of the building itself is a sight to behold.

Culinary Delights in Tours

No visit to Tours is complete without indulging in the local cuisine. The city is known for its gastronomic excellence, with numerous restaurants offering a taste of the Loire Valley. Le Saint Honoré (1 Rue de la Monnaie, 37000 Tours) is a must-visit, serving classic French dishes with a modern twist. For a more casual dining experience, head to La Deuvalière (18 Rue de la Monnaie, 37000 Tours), where you can enjoy delicious regional specialties in a cozy setting.

Wine lovers will appreciate a visit to the surrounding vineyards. Just a short drive from Tours, the Vouvray wine region offers some of the finest white wines in France. Book a tour and tasting at Domaine Huet (11 Rue de la Croix Buissée, 37210 Vouvray) to savor their exceptional Chenin Blanc wines.

Parks and Green Spaces

Tours is a city that values its green spaces. Take a leisurely stroll through the Jardin des Prébendes d'Oé (Rue Roger Salengro, 37000 Tours), a beautifully landscaped park with winding paths, flowerbeds, and a tranquil pond. It's the perfect spot for a relaxing afternoon.

For a more expansive natural escape, visit the Parc de la Gloriette (Rue du Colombier, 37200 Tours). This large park offers walking trails, picnic areas, and a scenic lake. It's an ideal location for families and nature enthusiasts.

Practical Information

Tours is well-connected by train, with regular services to Paris, making it an easy day trip or a perfect base for exploring the Loire Valley. The city's public transportation system, including buses and trams, is efficient and convenient for getting around.

When planning your stay, consider booking a room at the Hotel Oceania L'Univers Tours (5 Boulevard Heurteloup, 37000 Tours). This historic hotel combines modern amenities with classic charm, providing a comfortable and luxurious stay.

Blois: Royal History and Architectural Marvels

The Majestic Château de Blois

Your journey begins at the Château de Blois, located at 6 Place du Château. This stunning castle is a masterpiece of architecture, featuring four distinct wings, each built during different periods and reflecting a variety of styles. The Gothic wing, commissioned by King Louis XII, introduces you to the medieval origins of the château. As you move to the Renaissance wing, you'll marvel at the intricate details and ornate designs commissioned by Francis I. The Classical wing, added by Gaston d'Orléans, showcases the evolution of architectural tastes.

The château is not just about its exterior beauty; its interiors are equally mesmerizing. The opulent rooms, filled with period furniture and elaborate tapestries, provide a glimpse into the lavish lifestyles of the French monarchy. Don't miss the grand spiral staircase, a true architectural marvel, which seems to float effortlessly within its structure.

The House of Magic

Just across from the château at 1 Place du Château is La Maison de la Magie (The House of Magic). This unique museum pays homage to Jean-Eugène Robert-Houdin, the famous French illusionist born in Blois. The museum's six levels are filled with interactive exhibits, automata, and optical illusions that delight both children and adults. Every hour, the museum's façade comes alive with a whimsical dragon show, captivating onlookers.

St. Louis Cathedral

A short walk from the château, at Place Saint-Louis, stands the St. Louis Cathedral. This Gothic-style cathedral, rebuilt in the 17th century, is known for its stunning stained glass windows that narrate the story of Blois's past. The tranquility of the cathedral's interior, combined with its impressive architecture, makes it a must-visit for those seeking a moment of reflection.

Exploring the Old Town

The old town of Blois is a maze of narrow, winding streets, each filled with charming shops, cafes, and half-timbered houses. Wander through Rue du Commerce, a bustling street where you can find everything from artisanal chocolates at Chocolaterie Max Vauché (24 Rue du Commerce) to unique souvenirs. The Place Louis XII is a perfect spot to relax with a coffee and watch the world go by.

Musée des Beaux-Arts

Art enthusiasts should not miss the Musée des Beaux-Arts, located within the château itself. This museum houses an impressive collection of paintings, sculptures, and decorative arts spanning several centuries. Highlights include works by Rubens, Ingres, and Boucher. The museum also frequently hosts temporary exhibitions, adding a contemporary twist to its classical collection.

Blois Market

For an authentic taste of local life, visit the Blois Market held on Saturday mornings at Place Louis XII. Here, you can mingle with locals and sample regional specialties such as goat cheese, fresh baguettes, and Loire Valley wines. The vibrant atmosphere and the array of fresh produce and local delicacies make it a feast for the senses.

Nighttime Spectacle

As evening falls, return to the Château de Blois for the Son et Lumière (Sound and Light) show. This spectacular event, held from April to September, uses the château's façades as a canvas to project stunning visuals accompanied by a dramatic narrative. The show brings to life the historical events that shaped Blois and the lives of its royal residents.

Saumur: The Home of Cadre Noir and Sparkling Wines

The Cadre Noir: A Legacy of Equestrian Excellence

One cannot mention Saumur without celebrating the prestigious Cadre Noir. The French National Riding School, École Nationale d'Équitation, located at Avenue de l'École Nationale d'Équitation, 49400 Saumur, is home to this elite corps of riders who are dedicated to preserving and promoting classical dressage. Founded in 1814, the Cadre Noir is a symbol of French equestrian heritage and excellence.

Visitors to Saumur can witness the artistry of these equestrian masters through captivating public performances and tours. The "Gala du Cadre Noir" showcases intricate dressage routines, demonstrating the deep bond between rider and horse. The school also offers guided tours where you can explore the stables, training arenas, and learn about the rigorous training regime and history of the Cadre Noir. The annual open days, typically held in spring, provide an immersive experience with behind-the-scenes access to the training facilities and an opportunity to meet the riders and their magnificent horses.

Sparkling Wines: The Taste of Saumur

Saumur's vineyards are another jewel in its crown. The town is part of the Loire Valley wine region, famous for its exceptional sparkling wines, known as Crémant de Loire. The unique terroir, with its tuffeau limestone soil, provides ideal conditions for grape cultivation.

A visit to Saumur is incomplete without a tour of its wineries. One of the most renowned is the Maison Bouvet-Ladubay, located at 11 Rue Jean Ackerman, 49400 Saint-Hilaire-Saint-Florent. Established in 1851, this historic winery offers guided tours of its vast cellars, carved into the limestone hills. The tours culminate in a tasting session, where you can savor their exquisite Crémant de Loire and learn about the traditional méthode champenoise used in its production.

Another must-visit is Langlois-Chateau, found at 3 Rue Léopold Palustre, 49400 Saumur. This winery is known for its comprehensive tours, which include a visit to the vineyards, a walk through the cellars, and an informative session on the wine-making process. Their tasting sessions feature a variety of wines, from crisp whites to robust reds, showcasing the diversity of the region's produce.

For those looking to delve deeper into the world of Saumur wines, the Wine Museum, Musée du Champignon, located at Route de Gennes, 49350 Saumur, offers an extensive collection of wine-related artifacts and exhibits. This museum provides insight into the history of winemaking in the region, as well as the importance of mushrooms in the local agriculture, another product grown in the limestone caves.

Exploring Saumur's Historic and Cultural Sights

Beyond its equestrian and viticulture fame, Saumur is a town steeped in history. The imposing Château de Saumur, perched on a hill overlooking the town, offers panoramic views of the Loire River. This castle, located at Montée du Fort, 49400 Saumur, has served various roles over the centuries, from a fortress to a residence and now houses the Musée de la Cavalerie, celebrating Saumur's military history.

Strolling through Saumur's old town, with its narrow streets lined with timber-framed houses and charming squares, transports visitors back in time. The Place Saint-Pierre, with its lively cafes and restaurants, is perfect for soaking in the local atmosphere. Nearby, the Romanesque Church of Saint-Pierre, dating back to the 12th century, is a testament to the town's rich architectural heritage.

Practical Tips for Visitors

When planning a visit to Saumur, consider staying in one of the town's charming accommodations, such as the Hôtel Saint-Pierre, located at 8 Rue Haute Saint-Pierre, 49400 Saumur. This boutique hotel offers a blend of historic charm and modern comfort, making it an ideal base for exploring the town and its surroundings.

Saumur is well-connected by train, with regular services from Paris, Tours, and Angers. Once in town, renting a bike is a popular option for exploring the scenic Loire Valley countryside and nearby vineyards.

Orléans: Joan of Arc's Legacy

The Story of Joan of Arc in Orléans

Joan of Arc, or Jeanne d'Arc, is celebrated as the "Maid of Orléans" for her pivotal role in lifting the siege of the city during the Hundred Years' War. In 1429, at the age of 17, she led French forces to a momentous victory against the English, marking a turning point in the war. This victory not only saved Orléans but also paved the way for the coronation of Charles VII, restoring French confidence and national pride.

Exploring the Historic Sites

Start your journey at the Maison de Jeanne d'Arc (3 Place du Général de Gaulle, 45000 Orléans). This museum is dedicated to her life and legacy, housed in a faithfully reconstructed building where Joan stayed during the siege. Interactive exhibits and multimedia presentations bring her story to life, providing a deep understanding of her impact on Orléans and France.

A short walk from the museum leads you to the Cathédrale Sainte-Croix (Place Sainte-Croix, 45000 Orléans), a stunning Gothic cathedral where Joan attended mass. The cathedral's imposing façade and intricate stained glass windows, some depicting scenes from Joan's life, are breathtaking. Inside, take a moment to admire the soaring nave and the beautiful chapels.

Next, visit the Place du Martroi, the city's main square, where a magnificent equestrian statue of Joan of Arc stands. Sculpted by Denis Foyatier in 1855, this statue is a powerful symbol of her enduring legacy. The square itself is a bustling hub, surrounded by cafes and shops, perfect for a leisurely break.

Annual Joan of Arc Festival

Each year, Orléans honors its heroine with the Fêtes de Jeanne d'Arc, held from late April to early May. The festival features historical reenactments, parades, concerts, and a vibrant market. The highlight is the procession that traces Joan's steps through the city, culminating in a grand ceremony at the cathedral. Participating in this festival offers a unique opportunity to experience the city's deep-rooted traditions and community spirit.

Modern Orléans: Blending History with Vibrancy

While Joan of Arc's legacy is a significant draw, Orléans is a vibrant city that seamlessly blends its rich history with contemporary charm. Stroll along the banks of the Loire River, where modern cafes and restaurants line the picturesque promenades. The Musée des Beaux-Arts (1 Rue Fernand Rabier, 45000 Orléans) is another must-visit, showcasing an impressive collection of European art from the 15th to the 20th centuries.

For a taste of local cuisine, head to Les P'tits Instants (14 Rue de la Poterne, 45000 Orléans), a charming bistro known for its seasonal dishes and warm atmosphere. Don't miss trying the local specialty, Cotignac d'Orléans, a quince jelly treat that has been enjoyed since medieval times.

Practical Information

Orléans is easily accessible by train, with regular services from Paris, making it a convenient day trip or a pleasant addition to a longer Loire Valley itinerary. The city is well-connected by public transport, but its compact size makes it perfect for exploring on foot.

Best Villages to Experience Traditional Loire Valley Life

1. Montsoreau

Montsoreau is a picturesque village that sits gracefully on the banks of the Loire River. The village is dominated by the stunning Château de Montsoreau, the only château built directly in the riverbed. Walking through Montsoreau's narrow streets, you'll find beautifully preserved stone houses, quaint cafes, and local artisan shops. Don't miss the Sunday morning market where locals gather to buy fresh produce, cheeses, and other regional specialties. For an unforgettable dining experience, head to La Marine de Loire (9 Rue du Château, 49730 Montsoreau) where you can savor exquisite local dishes with a view of the river.

2. Candes-Saint-Martin

Just a stone's throw from Montsoreau lies Candes-Saint-Martin, another jewel of the Loire Valley. This village is classified as one of the "Most Beautiful Villages of France." Its charm lies in its medieval architecture and scenic river views. The Collégiale Saint-Martin, a remarkable Romanesque church, is a must-visit. Stroll along the cobblestone streets, lined with flower-filled gardens, and stop by Le Bistroglo (1 Place de l'Église, 37500 Candes-Saint-Martin) for a taste of traditional cuisine served in a cozy troglodyte setting.

3. Chédigny

Chédigny is a village unlike any other in the Loire Valley. It is the only village in France to be designated as a "Remarkable Garden." Known as the "Village of Roses," Chédigny bursts into a riot of colors and fragrances every spring. Over 1,000 rose bushes adorn the village, making it a paradise for flower lovers. Take a leisurely walk through the blooming streets and enjoy a meal at Le Clos aux Roses (8 Rue du Lavoir, 37310 Chédigny), a charming restaurant offering delicious local fare in a floral setting.

4. Crissay-sur-Manse

Crissay-sur-Manse is a quintessential Loire Valley village that seems frozen in time. Nestled in the heart of the countryside, it is surrounded by rolling hills and vineyards. The village is dotted with Renaissance houses, a 15th-century church, and the ruins of an old château. Visit the village during one of its many local festivals to experience the vibrant community spirit. Enjoy a glass of the region's famous wine at Les Caves de Crissay (15 Rue Principale, 37220 Crissay-sur-Manse), where you can also sample locally produced charcuterie and cheeses.

5. Lavardin

Lavardin is another "Most Beautiful Villages of France" member, known for its medieval charm and historic ruins. The village is overlooked by the remains of a 12th-century castle, which offers panoramic views of the surrounding landscape. Wander through Lavardin's enchanting streets, where half-timbered houses and old stone buildings transport you back in time. The Eglise Saint-Genest, with its striking frescoes, is a highlight. After exploring, relax at the Auberge de Lavardin (9 Rue du Château, 41800 Lavardin) and indulge in traditional dishes made from fresh, local ingredients.

6. Montrésor

Montrésor, set on the banks of the Indrois River, is a picture-perfect village that brims with history and charm. The imposing Château de Montrésor, with its Renaissance and Gothic architecture, is a must-visit. The village's narrow lanes, lined with historic houses and blooming flowers, lead you to the Collegiate Church of Saint John the Baptist. For a taste of village life, visit during the summer months when local festivals fill the streets with music, dance, and culinary delights. Dine at La Gerbe d'Or (12 Rue du Château, 37460 Montrésor) for a meal that perfectly captures the essence of the Loire Valley.

Chapter 3: Wine and Gastronomy

The Vineyards of the Loire: A Guide to Wine Regions

Sancerre and Pouilly-Fumé

Begin your wine journey in the eastern part of the Loire Valley, home to the renowned Sancerre and Pouilly-Fumé appellations. Nestled on the hills overlooking the Loire River, these vineyards are famed for their exceptional Sauvignon Blanc. The terroir here, characterized by limestone and flint soils, imparts a unique minerality to the wines.

Must-Visit Wineries:

Domaine Vacheron (3 Rue du Carrou, 18300 Sancerre): Known for its organic and biodynamic practices, Domaine Vacheron offers an intimate look into sustainable winemaking. Their crisp, mineral-driven Sauvignon Blancs are a highlight.

Domaine Didier Dagueneau (4 La Fougère, 58150 Saint-Andelain): This iconic Pouilly-Fumé producer is revered for its meticulous winemaking and distinctive flinty character in its wines. A tasting here is a must for any serious wine enthusiast.

Vouvray and Montlouis-sur-Loire

Travel westward to Vouvray and Montlouis-sur-Loire, where Chenin Blanc reigns supreme. These appellations produce a wide range of styles, from dry and sparkling to sweet and luscious dessert wines. The clay-limestone soils and cool climate provide ideal conditions for growing Chenin Blanc, resulting in wines with remarkable acidity and aging potential.

Must-Visit Wineries:

Domaine Huet (11 Rue de la Croix Buisée, 37210 Vouvray): A pioneer in biodynamic viticulture, Domaine Huet is renowned for its age-worthy Vouvray wines. Their estate, with its ancient cellars and picturesque vineyards, offers an unforgettable tasting experience.

Frantz Saumon (36 Rue de la Bourdaisière, 37270 Montlouis-sur-Loire): Known for his natural winemaking approach, Frantz Saumon crafts expressive and terroir-driven Chenin Blancs. The winery's laid-back atmosphere makes it a perfect stop for wine lovers.

Chinon and Bourgueil

For red wine aficionados, the Chinon and Bourgueil regions are a haven. Located in the heart of the Loire Valley, these appellations are celebrated for their Cabernet Franc. The wines here range from light and fruity to rich and robust, often displaying notes of red berries, herbs, and earthy undertones.

Must-Visit Wineries:

Domaine Bernard Baudry (12 Rue du Collège, 37500 Cravant-les-Coteaux): This family-run estate is a benchmark for Chinon wines. Their organic vineyards and minimalist winemaking approach produce elegant and complex Cabernet Francs.

Domaine de la Chevalerie (83 Rue de la Galottière, 37140 Restigné): In Bourgueil, this historic estate dates back to the 17th century. The Caslot family produces age-worthy Cabernet Francs that beautifully express the region's terroir.

Anjou and Saumur

As you venture further west, the Anjou and Saumur regions offer a delightful mix of wine styles. Anjou is known for its rosé wines, particularly Rosé d'Anjou, as well as its robust reds made from Cabernet Franc. Saumur, on the other hand, is renowned for its sparkling wines and elegant whites.

Must-Visit Wineries:

Château de Plaisance (19 Rue de la Gabelle, 49320 Thouarcé): This biodynamic estate in Anjou produces an impressive range of wines, from vibrant rosés to complex reds. The château's scenic setting adds to the charm of the tasting experience.

Domaine des Roches Neuves (95 Rue Haute Saint-Vincent, 49400 Varrains): In Saumur, Thierry Germain's estate is a standout. His meticulously crafted wines, especially the sparkling Crémant de Loire and Chenin Blancs, are a testament to the region's quality.

Wine Tasting Tours: Where and How

Starting Your Journey: Planning and Logistics

Begin your wine tasting journey by planning your itinerary. The Loire Valley stretches over 600 miles, so focusing on specific sub-regions can help maximize your experience. Consider renting a car for flexibility or joining an organized tour for convenience. Many tours offer hotel pick-ups, making it easy to explore without worrying about navigation or driving after tastings.

Must-Visit Vineyards and Wineries

1. Domaine Vacheron, Sancerre

Start in the eastern Loire with a visit to Domaine Vacheron in Sancerre, known for its exceptional Sauvignon Blanc. The Vacheron family has been producing organic wines here for generations. The vineyard offers guided tours where you can walk through the lush vines and learn about biodynamic farming practices. End with a tasting session in their modern, welcoming tasting room.

Address: 4 Rue de la Panneterie, 18300 Sancerre

2. Château de la Grille, Chinon

In the central Loire, head to Château de la Grille in Chinon. This 15th-century estate is not only a visual treat but also produces some of the finest Cabernet Franc in the region. The château offers detailed tours of its historic cellars, followed by a tasting of their robust reds and elegant rosés. Enjoy the serene garden views as you savor each glass.

Address: La Grille, 37500 Chinon

3. Domaine des Baumard, Rochefort-sur-Loire

Move westward to Domaine des Baumard in Rochefort-sur-Loire, celebrated for its exquisite Chenin Blanc. The

Baumard family has crafted wines here since 1634. Their tour includes a visit to the ancient tuffeau stone cellars, providing a cool respite as you sample their acclaimed Savennières and Coteaux du Layon.

Address: Le Logis de la Giraudière, 49190 Rochefort-sur-Loire

Tips for an Enjoyable Experience

Make Appointments: While some wineries welcome walk-ins, many require appointments. Booking in advance ensures a personalized and unrushed experience.

Pace Yourself: With numerous tastings, it's easy to become overwhelmed. Sip slowly, take notes, and stay hydrated. Many wineries offer spittoons—use them to pace yourself without overindulging.

Local Guides: Consider hiring a local guide. Their expertise can provide deeper insights into the wines and the history of the region. Plus, they often have insider access to private tastings.

Lunch Stops: Plan your route with lunch breaks at local bistros or vineyard restaurants. For instance, Le Bouchon in Chinon offers a delightful menu of local specialties paired with regional wines.

Address: 23 Place du Général de Gaulle, 37500 Chinon

Accommodations: Stay at vineyard accommodations for an immersive experience. Château de Noizay in Vouvray offers luxurious rooms within a short distance of top vineyards.

Address: 124 Promenade de Waulsort, 37210 Noizay

Beyond Tastings: Wine Festivals and Events

Time your visit to coincide with local wine festivals. The "Fête des Vendanges" in Montmartre, although held in Paris, celebrates Loire wines with great fanfare. The "VitiLoire" festival in Tours, held annually in May, showcases the best of Loire Valley wines with tastings, workshops, and gourmet food pairings.

Bringing It Home: Wine Shipping

Most wineries offer shipping services, allowing you to send your favorite bottles home without hassle. Be sure to check the import regulations of your home country to ensure a smooth process.

Local Cuisine: Must-Try Dishes and Where to Find Them

Tarte Tatin

A delightful upside-down caramelized apple tart, Tarte Tatin originated from the nearby Sologne region. This sweet treat is a perfect example of simple ingredients transformed into something extraordinary. Pâtisserie Bigot in Amboise (2 Rue Nationale, 37400 Amboise) serves an exquisite version, where the apples are tender, and the pastry is perfectly crisp. Enjoy it with a cup of their fine coffee while you take in views of the Château d'Amboise.

Rillettes de Tours

Rillettes de Tours is a rich, savory spread made from slow-cooked pork, typically enjoyed with crusty bread. For an authentic taste, head to La Maison des Halles in Tours (5 Place des Halles, 37000 Tours). Their rillettes are melt-in-your-mouth tender, seasoned to perfection, and epitomize traditional Loire Valley charcuterie.

Andouillette

This distinctive sausage made from pork intestines may be an acquired taste, but it's a beloved local specialty. Try it at Bistrot des Belles Caves in Tours (18 Place Foire le Roi,

37000 Tours), where the chefs prepare it with a mustard sauce that balances its strong flavors. Pair it with a glass of Vouvray for a classic Loire Valley experience.

Beuchelle à la Tourangelle

A hearty dish featuring sweetbreads and kidneys in a creamy mushroom sauce, Beuchelle à la Tourangelle is a true delicacy. Les Halles de Tours (Place Gaston Paillhou, 37000 Tours) offers an excellent version, cooked to perfection and served with fresh local vegetables. The market setting adds to the charm, making your meal feel authentically local.

Pithiviers

Pithiviers is a pastry filled with almond cream, and sometimes fruits or meats. It's a delightful treat that showcases the region's baking prowess. La Chocolaterie Max Vauché in Bracieux (3 Rue de l'Église, 41250 Bracieux) is famous for its sweet almond Pithiviers, a perfect snack while exploring nearby Château de Chambord.

Poire Tapée

This unique dish involves pears that are dried, flattened, and then rehydrated, resulting in a concentrated sweet and tangy flavor. For the best Poire Tapée, visit Maison Hérin in Rivarennes (12 Rue des Ducs d'Aquitaine, 37190

Rivarennes), where they continue this traditional method with care and expertise. It's a true taste of the region's ingenuity in preserving fruits.

Sainte-Maure de Touraine

A staple of the Loire Valley's cheese selection, Sainte-Maure de Touraine is a goat cheese rolled in ash and marked with a piece of straw. Visit Fromagerie Hardy in Tours (Place des Halles, 37000 Tours) to sample some of the finest. The cheese is creamy with a subtle tang, perfect for a picnic along the Loire River.

Sandre en Sauce au Beurre Blanc

This dish features pike-perch from the Loire River, cooked in a buttery white wine sauce. L'Épicerie Gourmande in Saumur (17 Rue Saint-Jean, 49400 Saumur) serves a superb version, where the fish is tender and the sauce is luxuriously rich. Enjoy it with a local Saumur-Champigny wine.

Farmers' Markets: Fresh Produce and Artisan Goods

Tours Farmers' Market

Address: Boulevard Béranger, 37000 Tours, France

Market Days: Wednesdays and Saturdays, 7:00 AM - 1:00 PM

The Tours Farmers' Market is one of the largest and most diverse in the Loire Valley. Set against the backdrop of Boulevard Béranger, the market features an array of stalls offering everything from seasonal fruits and vegetables to regional specialties like rillettes and goat cheese. Arrive early to beat the crowds and enjoy a leisurely stroll as you sample freshly baked bread, pastries, and an assortment of charcuterie. Don't miss the vibrant flower stalls, where you can pick up a bouquet to brighten your day.

Amboise Market

Address: Place du Marché, 37400 Amboise, France

Market Days: Fridays and Sundays, 8:00 AM - 1:00 PM

Situated in the shadow of the stunning Château d'Amboise, the Amboise Market is a must-visit. This market is renowned for its high-quality produce and friendly atmosphere. On market days, the Place du Marché comes alive with vendors selling fresh fruits, vegetables, seafood, and an impressive selection of local wines. Be sure to try the famous fouées, a type of stuffed bread that is a local favorite. The market also offers a selection of handcrafted goods, including pottery and textiles, perfect for a unique souvenir.

Blois Market

Address: Place Louis XII, 41000 Blois, France

Market Days: Saturdays, 7:00 AM - 1:00 PM

The Blois Market, held in the historic Place Louis XII, is a bustling hub of activity. This market is particularly famous for its organic produce and artisanal cheeses. Stroll through the stalls and you'll find a delightful variety of seasonal fruits, vegetables, fresh fish, and meat. The cheese vendors are particularly noteworthy, offering a wide range of local cheeses such as Sainte-Maure de Touraine and Valençay. For a sweet treat, try the local honey and preserves, made from fruits grown in the surrounding orchards.

Saumur Market

Address: Place Saint-Pierre, 49400 Saumur, France

Market Days: Saturdays, 8:00 AM - 1:00 PM

In the charming town of Saumur, the market at Place Saint-Pierre is a highlight of the week. This market showcases the best of the region's produce, with an emphasis on organic and locally-sourced goods. From freshly picked asparagus in the spring to juicy plums and tomatoes in the summer, the produce here is as fresh as it gets. Saumur is also known for its sparkling wines, and many vendors offer tastings alongside their selection of bottles. Be sure to stop by the bakery stalls for a taste of the local brioche.

Loches Market

Address: Place de la Marne, 37600 Loches, France

Market Days: Wednesdays and Saturdays, 8:00 AM - 1:00 PM

The medieval town of Loches hosts a wonderful market in Place de la Marne. This market is smaller but offers a charming and intimate shopping experience. Vendors here are passionate about their products, which include organic vegetables, farm-fresh eggs, and homemade jams. The market also features local artisans selling handmade soaps, candles, and jewelry. Enjoy a leisurely morning here, chatting with the friendly vendors and sampling the delicious offerings.

Cooking Classes: Learn to Cook Like a Local

La Maison des Saveurs

Address: 1 Rue de la Roche, 37000 Tours, France

Phone: +33 2 47 05 12 05

La Maison des Saveurs in Tours is a renowned cooking school that offers hands-on classes focusing on the region's traditional dishes. Chef Claude Moreau, a local culinary expert, leads classes that delve into the preparation of classic Loire Valley dishes like rillettes, coq au vin, and tarte tatin. The intimate setting and personalized instruction ensure that you receive ample attention, and the classes often include a visit to the local market to select the freshest ingredients.

Atelier de Cuisine de La Table Ronde

Address: 24 Rue de l'Embourie, 49100 Angers, France

Phone: +33 2 41 87 54 54

Website: latableronde.com

Located in the heart of Angers, Atelier de Cuisine de La Table Ronde offers a range of cooking classes designed to immerse you in the local culinary culture. Here, you can learn to prepare a variety of dishes, from exquisite Loire Valley seafood to delicious pâtés and pastries. The classes are taught by Chef Sophie Dupont, who emphasizes using seasonal and local ingredients. Classes often end with a communal meal where you can enjoy the dishes you've prepared, paired with local wines.

Le Cooking Club du Val de Loire

Address: 5 Boulevard du Maréchal Leclerc, 37100 Tours, France

Phone: +33 2 47 61 38 74

Website: cooking-club-valdeloire.com

The Cooking Club du Val de Loire, located in Tours, offers a variety of cooking workshops that cater to different skill levels. The school specializes in traditional French cuisine with a focus on Loire Valley specialties. From making the perfect quiche Lorraine to crafting delicate croissants, their classes are designed to provide a thorough understanding of French culinary techniques. The hands-on approach ensures that you leave with both practical skills and a delicious meal.

Château de la Bourdaisière

Address: Château de la Bourdaisière, 37170 Montlouis-sur-Loire, France

Phone: +33 2 47 45 42 42

Website: chateaudelabourdaisiere.com

For a unique experience, consider a cooking class at the Château de la Bourdaisière, a historic castle surrounded by gardens. Here, you can take part in classes that focus on garden-to-table cooking, using ingredients freshly harvested from the château's own gardens. Chef Jean-Luc Charbonnier leads these classes, offering insight into how to prepare dishes that reflect the rich flavors of the Loire Valley's produce.

Tips for Your Cooking Class Experience

Book in Advance: Classes can fill up quickly, especially during peak tourist season. It's advisable to book your spot well in advance to ensure availability.

Dress Comfortably: Wear comfortable clothing and closed-toe shoes, as you'll be spending time in a working kitchen.

Ask Questions: Don't hesitate to ask your instructors about techniques, ingredients, and local culinary traditions. They're usually eager to share their knowledge.

Bring a Notebook: Jotting down notes during the class can be helpful when you're recreating the recipes at home.

Chapter 4: Outdoor Adventures

Cycling the Loire à Vélo: The Ultimate Biking Experience

Route Overview

The Loire à Vélo is a well-marked, mostly flat route that is suitable for cyclists of all levels. It stretches from Cuffy, near Nevers, to Saint-Brevin-les-Pins on the Atlantic coast, with the central section passing through the heart of the Loire Valley. This guide will focus on the most enchanting part of the trail, from Orléans to Angers, which is rich in historical sites and natural beauty.

Key Highlights

Orléans to Sully-sur-Loire

Begin your adventure in Orléans, a city steeped in history and known for its connection to Joan of Arc. Start at the Hôtel de Ville (Place du Martroi), where you can rent a bike from Cycles de l'Orléanais at 2 Rue de la République. As you cycle out of Orléans, the route takes you along the scenic banks of the Loire River, passing lush vineyards and picturesque countryside. Stop at Château de Sully-sur-Loire (Place de l'Étape, 45600 Sully-sur-Loire) to explore this impressive medieval fortress and enjoy its tranquil gardens.

Sully-sur-Loire to Blois

Continuing on, make your way to Blois, a city renowned for its rich history and architectural heritage. The trail offers stunning views of the Loire, with plenty of opportunities to pause and admire the landscape. In Blois, visit the Château de Blois (6 Place du Château, 41000 Blois), a magnificent castle that was a favorite residence of French kings. The castle's ornate façades and beautifully preserved rooms offer a glimpse into the royal past.

Blois to Amboise

As you pedal towards Amboise, the route is dotted with charming villages and vineyards. In Amboise, make sure to visit the Château d'Amboise (Montée de l'Impérial, 37400 Amboise), a historic royal residence where Leonardo da Vinci spent his final years. The château provides spectacular views of the Loire Valley and an intriguing look at Renaissance art and history.

Amboise to Tours

The final stretch to Tours takes you through rolling countryside and vibrant vineyards. Tours itself is a lively city with a rich cultural scene. Visit the Place Plumereau, a bustling square surrounded by medieval buildings and cafes. For bike rental in Tours, check out Tours à Vélo at 6 Rue de la Préfecture.

Practical Tips

Bike Rentals and Repairs: Most major towns along the route offer bike rental services. Ensure your bike is in good condition before starting and carry a basic repair kit.

Accommodation: Consider staying in local guesthouses or charming bed-and-breakfasts for a more authentic experience. Book accommodations in advance, especially during peak season.

Local Cuisine: Take advantage of the opportunity to sample local wines and cuisine at regional restaurants and markets. Try specialties like goat cheese and Loire Valley wines.

Walking and Hiking Trails: Discover Nature's Beauty

1. Loire à Vélo Path

Location: From Nevers to Saint-Brevin-les-Pins

Description: While primarily known as a cycling route, the Loire à Vélo Path is also ideal for walkers. This trail follows the banks of the Loire River, offering stunning views of the water and the surrounding countryside. The path passes through charming towns like Amboise and Blois, where you can take a break and explore local attractions. Along the way, you'll encounter vineyards, historic sites, and lush forests. A recommended segment is the stretch between Tours and Amboise, which features particularly picturesque views and manageable distances.

Tip: Start your journey at the Tours Tourist Office for maps and local advice. (Tourist Office Address: 78 Rue Bernard Palissy, 37000 Tours)

2. Forests of Amboise

Location: Amboise, near Château d'Amboise

Description: The Forest of Amboise, located just south of the Château d'Amboise, offers a network of trails perfect for a ely hike or an invigorating walk. The forest is characterized by its ancient trees, serene pathways, and tranquil atmosphere. The trails vary in difficulty, with some leading to scenic viewpoints over the Loire River. One notable trail is the "Chemin des Promesses," which takes you through lush greenery and offers panoramic views of the surrounding countryside.

Tip: Parking is available near the Château d'Amboise, and trails are well-marked. (Château d'Amboise Address: Montée de l'Emir Abd el Kader, 37400 Amboise)

3. Château de Chaumont-sur-Loire Gardens

Location: Chaumont-sur-Loire

Description: While the Château de Chaumont-sur-Loire is famous for its gardens and the annual International Garden Festival, the surrounding grounds also offer excellent walking trails. The "Promenade du Vignoble" trail winds through the vineyards and gardens, providing a delightful combination of nature and horticulture. The trail is relatively easy, making it accessible for all fitness levels, and offers stunning views of the château and the Loire River.

Tip: Visit the château and gardens for a full experience. (Château Address: 41150 Chaumont-sur-Loire)

4. Sologne Region Trails

Location: Sologne, south of the Loire Valley

Description: The Sologne region, known for its dense forests and wetland areas, provides a range of hiking options. The "Circuit de la Forêt" is a popular trail that explores the heart of the Sologne Forest. This trail takes you through ancient oak woods, past serene lakes, and offers the chance to spot local wildlife. It's a great option for those looking to experience the natural diversity of the Loire Valley.

Tip: The Sologne region is best explored with a local map or guide, as trails can vary in difficulty. (Local Tourism Office Address: 5 Rue des Champs, 41300 Romorantin-Lanthenay)

5. Parc Floral de la Source

Location: Orléans

Description: For a more relaxed walking experience, the Parc Floral de la Source in Orléans offers beautifully landscaped gardens and easy trails. The park features a variety of floral displays, thematic gardens, and serene walking paths. It's an ideal spot for a peaceful stroll, with opportunities to enjoy seasonal blooms and tranquil water features.

Tip: The park is accessible year-round, and guided tours are available. (Park Address: 45100 Orléans)

Hot Air Balloon Rides: A Bird's Eye View of the Valley

Choosing Your Balloon Ride Experience

Several reputable companies offer hot air balloon rides in the Loire Valley, each promising an unforgettable adventure. One highly recommended provider is Loire Ballons, based in Tours. They have been operating for over 20 years and offer a range of flight options to suit different preferences.

Loire Ballons

Address: 7 Rue du Château, 37100 Tours, France

Phone: +33 2 47 05 00 02

Website: loireballons.com

Another excellent choice is Montgolfière de la Loire, which operates from Saumur. Their flights are known for exceptional service and spectacular views.

Montgolfière de la Loire

Address: 1 Rue des Écoles, 49400 Saumur, France

Phone: +33 2 41 67 29 10

Website: montgolfieredelaire.com

What to Expect

Pre-Flight Preparations

Before your flight, you'll typically meet at the launch site early in the morning, just before sunrise. This is when the winds are calmest, providing the smoothest ride. After a safety briefing and a brief explanation of how the balloon operates, you'll have the opportunity to help inflate the balloon—a fascinating process that adds to the excitement of the experience.

The Flight

As the balloon lifts off, you'll be gently carried upwards, with the stunning vistas of the Loire Valley gradually unfolding beneath you. The serenity of floating high above the ground is complemented by the panoramic views of the valley's vineyards, historic towns, and the iconic châteaux such as Château de Chambord and Château de Chenonceau. The flight typically lasts between 45 minutes to an hour, depending on weather conditions and the specific package you choose.

Post-Flight Celebration

After landing, the adventure continues with a traditional celebration, often including a glass of champagne and a e of your flight. This moment provides an ...ity to reflect on the breathtaking views and the unique experience you've just enjoyed.

Tips for a Memorable Flight

Dress Comfortably: Wear layered clothing suitable for both cool mornings and warmer temperatures as the sun rises. Closed-toe shoes are essential.

Camera Ready: Ensure your camera or smartphone is fully charged to capture the stunning aerial views.

Book in Advance: Hot air balloon rides are popular, especially in peak seasons. Booking ahead will secure your spot and allow you to choose the best time for your flight.

A hot air balloon ride over the Loire Valley of

River Activities: Kayaking and Canoeing on the Loire

Choosing Your Route

One of the most popular sections for kayaking and canoeing is the stretch between Château de Chaumont-sur-Loire and Amboise. This segment offers a mix of serene waters and gentle rapids, with stunning views of some of the Loire Valley's most iconic châteaux. Launching from Chaumont-sur-Loire (Place du Château, 41150 Chaumont-sur-Loire), you'll paddle past lush vineyards, rolling meadows, and the picturesque town of Montlivault.

For a more adventurous experience, consider the section from Sully-sur-Loire to Châteauneuf-sur-Loire. This 20-kilometer stretch offers a combination of peaceful stretches and exciting currents. Sully-sur-Loire (Place de la République, 45600 Sully-sur-Loire) is a great starting point, and you can arrange rentals through Aventure Loire (12 Quai du Château, 45600 Sully-sur-Loire), a local outfitter known for their comprehensive services and friendly guides.

What to Expect

As you paddle, you'll glide past lush landscapes and historic towns, with occasional glimpses of wildlife such as herons, kingfishers, and even the rare otter. The Loire is relatively shallow in many areas, making it accessible for beginners, though some experience with river paddling is beneficial. The calm waters near the Château de Chenonceau (37150 Chenonceaux) provide a serene backdrop, allowing you to marvel at the castle's reflection in the river.

Practical Tips

Rental and Tours: For those new to kayaking or canoeing, consider booking a guided tour. Loire Aventure (36 Rue de la

République, 37000 Tours) offers guided tours and rentals with all necessary equipment included. They also provide valuable safety instructions and local insights.

Safety: Always wear a life jacket and check the weather before heading out. The Loire's currents can be unpredictable, especially after rain. If you're planning on paddling on your own, ensure you have a map and a means of communication in case of emergencies.

Permits and Fees: Most sections of the Loire do not require a permit for recreational paddling, but it's always good to check with local authorities or rental companies for any specific regulations.

Best Time to Go: Spring and early autumn are ideal for paddling on the Loire. The weather is mild, and the river levels are usually stable. Summer can be quite busy, and winter can bring challenging conditions.

Scenic Stops

Château de Chaumont-sur-Loire: Aside from its famous gardens, this château offers beautiful riverside views. Take a moment to enjoy the setting before continuing your journey.

Amboise: As you approach Amboise (3 Rue des Forges, 37400 Amboise), the imposing Château d'Amboise comes into view, offering a dramatic end to your paddle.

Chapter 5: Arts and Culture

Museums and Galleries: Art and History

Musée des Beaux-Arts de Tours

5 Place François Sicard, 37000 Tours

The Musée des Beaux-Arts de Tours, situated in the heart of Tours, is a jewel for art lovers. Housed in a former bishop's palace, this museum boasts an impressive collection of European art spanning from the Middle Ages to the 19th century. Highlights include works by French masters like Delacroix and Boucher, as well as an extensive collection of Dutch and Flemish paintings. The museum's charming courtyard, with its serene garden, provides a peaceful retreat amidst the art.

Musée d'Art et d'Histoire de Chinon

Place du Général de Gaulle, 37500 Chinon

In Chinon, the Musée d'Art et d'Histoire offers a captivating glimpse into the region's past. Located in the heart of this historic town, the museum's exhibits range from archaeological finds to medieval weaponry and Renaissance art. The museum's collection is particularly strong in items related to the town's role in the Hundred Years' War and the reign of Joan of Arc. Don't miss the beautifully preserved medieval manuscripts and the intriguing dioramas that bring local history to life.

Château de Blois – Musée des Beaux-Arts

6 Place du Château, 41000 Blois

The Château de Blois, while renowned for its architectural splendor, also houses a remarkable museum within its walls. The Musée des Beaux-Arts at Blois features an eclectic collection of artworks that include pieces from the Renaissance to the 20th century. The museum's galleries are adorned with paintings, sculptures, and tapestries, many of which reflect the history of the château and its former inhabitants. The integration of the museum within the château's historical context creates a unique and immersive experience.

La Maison de la Magie Robert-Houdin

1 Place du Château, 41000 Blois

For a more whimsical take on art and history, La Maison de la Magie in Blois celebrates the legacy of Robert-Houdin, a pioneer of modern magic and illusion. The museum, dedicated to Houdin's life and works, features an impressive collection of magical apparatus, posters, and personal memorabilia. The interactive exhibits and magical performances make it a delightful stop for visitors of all ages.

Musée de la Société des Sciences Naturelles et d'Archéologie de Tours

1 Rue des Ursulines, 37000 Tours

This lesser-known gem in Tours offers a fascinating look into natural history and archaeology. The museum's diverse collections include fossils, minerals, and ancient artifacts from across the Loire Valley. The exhibits provide context to the region's historical and geological evolution, making it a valuable stop for those interested in the natural sciences.

Musée de la Préhistoire du Grand-Pressigny

2 Place de la Mairie, 37350 Le Grand-Pressigny

For those intrigued by prehistoric art, the Musée de la Préhistoire in Le Grand-Pressigny is a must-visit. The museum is renowned for its extensive collection of prehistoric tools and artifacts, particularly those from the local area. The exhibits offer insight into early human life in the Loire Valley, including tools and artwork from the Neolithic period.

Festivals and Events: Celebrating Local Traditions

1. Fête de la Musique (June 21)

Celebrated nationwide, the Fête de la Musique transforms the Loire Valley into an open-air concert venue. In cities like Tours and Blois, musicians of all genres—from classical to contemporary—perform on streets, in parks, and at various venues, creating a joyous atmosphere that attracts locals and tourists alike. This event, held in honor of the summer solstice, offers a perfect opportunity to experience the region's lively music scene and enjoy spontaneous performances as you stroll through the historic city centers.

2. Festival des Châteaux en Fête (July)

This annual festival, held throughout July, celebrates the grandeur of the Loire Valley's châteaux with a series of events including medieval reenactments, art exhibitions, and themed tours. Major castles such as Château de Chambord and Château de Chenonceau open their gates for special tours and performances that highlight their historical significance. For an immersive experience, you can witness traditional jousting tournaments and falconry displays, which bring the history of these magnificent estates to life.

3. La Saint-Vincent Tournante (Last Weekend in January)

Hosted in the charming village of Santenay, La Saint-Vincent Tournante is a winter wine festival dedicated to celebrating Burgundy wines, including those produced in the Loire Valley. This vibrant event features wine tastings, parades, and traditional music. Local winemakers showcase their best vintages, offering an excellent opportunity to sample regional wines and learn about the winemaking process. The festival also includes food stalls with regional specialties, making it a feast for the senses.

4. Les Fêtes de la Loire (August)

Taking place in Tours, Les Fêtes de la Loire is a spectacular celebration of the region's maritime heritage. The event features a grand parade of traditional boats on the Loire River, live music, and theatrical performances. The highlight is the colorful fireworks display over the river, which draws crowds from all over the region. It's a fantastic way to experience the local culture and enjoy a lively atmosphere on the banks of the Loire.

5. Festival des Jardins de Chaumont-sur-Loire (April to October)

Held annually at Château de Chaumont-sur-Loire, this festival is a must-visit for garden enthusiasts. The event showcases innovative garden designs and installations created by renowned landscape architects from around the world. Visitors can explore themed gardens, attend workshops, and gain inspiration from the stunning horticultural displays. The festival's location, with its breathtaking views over the Loire River, adds to the enchanting experience.

6. Fête de la Gastronomie (September)

The Fête de la Gastronomie, celebrated in various towns throughout the Loire Valley, is a tribute to French culinary excellence. This festival highlights local cuisine with food fairs, cooking demonstrations, and special menus at restaurants. In cities like Amboise and Saumur, you can sample traditional dishes prepared with local ingredients and participate in cooking classes to learn the secrets of Loire Valley cuisine.

Music and Performing Arts: The Best Venues and Performances

1. Théâtre de Tours – Tours

Located at 3 Place du Grand Marché, 37000 Tours, the Théâtre de Tours is a historic venue that has been a cornerstone of the local arts scene since its opening in 1866. This grand theater hosts a diverse array of performances, from classical music concerts and operas to contemporary theater and dance. The venue itself is an architectural gem, with its elegant façade and opulent interior providing the perfect backdrop for an evening of high culture. The theater's season typically runs from September to June, featuring both French and international artists. Be sure to check their website for the current schedule and ticket availability.

2. Le Vinci – Tours

Just a short walk from the Théâtre de Tours, Le Vinci is located at 31 Boulevard Heurteloup, 37000 Tours. This modern performance space, inaugurated in 1992, is known for its versatile design, accommodating everything from orchestral concerts to jazz performances and theater productions. Le Vinci is particularly renowned for its annual festival of classical music, the Festival de Musique Classique, which attracts top musicians from around the world. The venue also hosts a variety of events throughout the year, so it's worth checking their calendar for upcoming performances.

3. Château de Chaumont-sur-Loire – Chaumont-sur-Loire

For a unique experience, visit the Château de Chaumont-sur-Loire, located at 41150 Chaumont-sur-Loire. This stunning château, which hosts the annual International Garden Festival, also offers a series of classical music concerts during the summer months. The performances take place in the château's beautiful Salle des Fêtes, providing an enchanting setting with its historic ambiance and stunning views of the Loire River. Concerts are often held in collaboration with the Orchestre Symphonique de Tours, ensuring high-quality musical experiences.

4. Les Concerts de l'Hostel Dieu – Blois

Situated at 5 Rue du Commerce, 41000 Blois, the Hostel Dieu is a historic building that now serves as a venue for the Les Concerts de l'Hostel Dieu. This series of classical music concerts is held in a beautifully restored chapel, offering an intimate and acoustically superb setting for performances. The concerts typically feature a mix of solo and chamber music, performed by both emerging and established artists. The series runs from May to September, and tickets can be purchased directly from the venue or through local tourism offices.

5. Festival de Musique de Chambord – Chambord

Held annually in the stunning Château de Chambord, 41250 Chambord, the Festival de Musique de Chambord is a must-attend event for classical music lovers. This festival, set against the backdrop of one of France's most iconic châteaux, showcases a range of musical genres, including baroque, classical, and contemporary works. The festival usually takes place in July, and its performances are held in the château's grand Salle des Fêtes. It's an experience that combines the grandeur of the château with the beauty of live music, creating an unforgettable cultural event.

6. La Maison de la Magie – Blois

For a touch of magic and theatrical wonder, visit La Maison de la Magie, located at 1 Place du Château, 41000 Blois. This venue, dedicated to the art of magic and illusion, features regular performances that blend magic, theater, and music. It's an engaging experience for visitors of all ages and offers a unique glimpse into the world of magical arts. The performances are held throughout the year, with special shows during major festivals and holiday seasons.

Chapter 6: Family-Friendly Activities

Kid-Friendly Châteaux: Fun for the Whole Family

Château de Chambord

Address: 41250 Chambord, France

Website: chambord.org

Highlights: Known for its impressive Renaissance architecture, Château de Chambord is not just a feast for the eyes but also a playground for the imagination. Children will be delighted by the château's grand staircase, which seems to spiral endlessly, and its vast grounds, perfect for running and exploring. The château offers a treasure hunt activity designed specifically for kids, which makes discovering the castle's secrets a fun and interactive experience. Don't miss the chance to visit the on-site "Great Stables," where the kids can learn about the historical use of horses in the castle's daily life.

Château de Chenonceau

Address: 37150 Chenonceaux, France

Website: chenonceau.com

Highlights: Dubbed the "Ladies' Castle" due to its association with several influential women, Château de Chenonceau is enchanting for all ages. Children will love the château's picturesque gardens, which include a labyrinth and a fairy-tale-like maze. The château hosts seasonal workshops where kids can engage in crafts, archery, and period games. The "Les Enfants du Patrimoine" program offers special guided tours with interactive elements designed to capture the imagination of younger visitors.

Château de Cheverny

Address: 41700 Cheverny, France

Website: chateau-cheverny.fr

Highlights: Château de Cheverny is renowned for its well-preserved interiors and the impressive "Mosaic Garden." Children will be fascinated by the daily feeding of the hounds, a tradition that dates back centuries. The château also features a playful "Hergé's Tintin" exhibition, celebrating the famous comic series. The Tintin exhibit includes models and scenes from the adventures of Tintin, allowing children to step into the world of their favorite characters.

Château du Clos Lucé

Address: 2 Rue du Clos Lucé, 37400 Amboise, France

Website: closluce.com

Highlights: The final residence of Leonardo da Vinci, Château du Clos Lucé is perfect for children interested in science and inventions. The château offers interactive exhibits that showcase Leonardo's innovative designs and inventions. Kids can try out hands-on activities like building simple machines and exploring replicas of Leonardo's inventions. The beautiful gardens are also ideal for a picnic and offer space for children to play and explore.

Château de Villandry

Address: 3 Rue Principale, 37510 Villandry, France

Website: villandry.fr

Highlights: Famous for its stunning Renaissance gardens, Château de Villandry provides an immersive experience for families. The château's gardens include a maze that kids will love to navigate, and the "Garden of Eden" is a particularly enchanting spot for children. The château also hosts seasonal events such as garden workshops and educational tours tailored for young visitors.

Parks and Playgrounds: Let the Little Ones Run Wild

1. Parc des Mini-Châteaux, Amboise

Located at Parc des Mini-Châteaux, 37150 Amboise, this charming park is a miniature wonderland of the Loire Valley's most famous châteaux. Kids will love exploring the scaled-down versions of iconic castles like Château de Chambord and Château de Chenonceau, complete with interactive elements and educational displays. The park also features play areas, including climbing structures and swings, making it an ideal spot for a family outing. The surrounding gardens and picnic areas offer a pleasant setting for a break.

2. Parc Floral de la Source, Orléans

Situated at 1 Rue de la Source, 45000 Orléans, the Parc Floral de la Source is a beautifully landscaped park that provides a variety of activities for children. With expansive lawns, vibrant flower beds, and themed gardens, it's perfect for a leisurely stroll or a fun family picnic. The park features a large playground with slides, swings, and climbing frames. During the summer months, there are often special events and workshops aimed at engaging younger visitors.

3. Le Jardin des Fées, Château de Villandry

At Château de Villandry, 37510 Villandry, you'll find not only the stunning Renaissance gardens but also Le Jardin des Fées—a magical play area for children. Inspired by the château's enchanting gardens, this area includes themed play equipment that encourages imaginative play. Children can explore a castle-themed playground, enjoy the swings and slides, and take part in garden-themed games designed to stimulate their creativity and curiosity.

4. Parc du Château de Rochecotte, Langeais

Located at Château de Rochecotte, 37130 Langeais, this park is set in the grounds of a beautiful château. The expansive lawns and shaded areas provide a perfect setting for children to run around and play. The park features several playgrounds with modern equipment, including climbing walls and interactive play structures. Families can enjoy a picnic under the trees or explore the château's gardens, which offer a picturesque backdrop for a day out.

5. Parc de la Planchette, Tours

At 2 Rue de la Planchette, 37000 Tours, Parc de la Planchette is a local favorite for families. This park offers a mix of open spaces and well-equipped play areas, including swings, slides, and climbing frames. The park is also home to a small pond with ducks and other wildlife, which adds an educational element to your visit. The shaded paths and benches make it easy for parents to keep an eye on their children while enjoying the serene surroundings.

Zoos and Wildlife Parks: Close Encounters with Nature

1. ZooParc de Beauval

Located in Saint-Aignan-sur-Cher, ZooParc de Beauval is arguably the premier wildlife park in the Loire Valley. Spanning over 35 hectares, this park is home to more than 8,000 animals across 600 species, making it one of France's largest and most diverse zoos.

Address: 41110 Saint-Aignan-sur-Cher, France

Website: beauval.com

The zoo is renowned for its impressive collection, including giant pandas, white tigers, and a variety of primates. Visitors can explore themed areas like the African Savannah, the Amazonian Rainforest, and the Chinese Garden, each meticulously designed to mimic the animals' natural habitats. Highlights include the daily feeding sessions, educational talks, and interactive exhibits that offer an immersive experience for all ages.

2. Parc Animalier de la Haute-Touche

Situated in the heart of the Brenne Regional Nature Park, Parc Animalier de la Haute-Touche is a lesser-known gem for wildlife lovers. Covering 130 hectares, this park focuses on the conservation of European wildlife and offers a more tranquil experience compared to larger zoos.

Address: 36300 Azay-le-Ferron, France

Website: haute-touche.fr

The park is home to over 100 species, including wolves, wild boar, and European bison. Visitors can enjoy walking trails through the park's natural woodland and wetlands, providing a scenic and educational journey through native fauna. The park emphasizes conservation and offers insights into the ongoing efforts to protect endangered species.

3. La Maison de la Nature

La Maison de la Nature, located in the village of Chaumussay, offers a more intimate wildlife experience. While not a zoo in the traditional sense, this nature center provides an opportunity to learn about local wildlife and participate in hands-on educational activities.

Address: 37330 Chaumussay, France

Website: maison-nature.com

Visitors can explore the surrounding nature reserve and participate in guided walks, bird-watching tours, and workshops focused on wildlife conservation and ecology. The center is ideal for families looking to engage in nature-focused activities and learn about the region's biodiversity.

Tips for Visiting

Plan Ahead: Check the websites of each park for opening hours, ticket prices, and any special events or restrictions.

Comfortable Footwear: Many parks require extensive walking, so wear comfortable shoes and dress for the weather.

Respect Wildlife: Follow park rules and guidelines to ensure a safe and respectful visit for both the animals and yourself.

Interactive Museums: Learning Through Play

1. La Maison de la Magie (House of Magic)

Location: 1 Place du Château, 41000 Blois, France

Situated in the heart of Blois, La Maison de la Magie is a unique museum dedicated to the art of magic and illusion.

Housed in a 16th-century mansion with an enchanting view of the Château de Blois, this museum celebrates the life and work of Robert-Houdin, a renowned magician and inventor.

Upon entering, you'll be greeted by a whimsical collection of magical artifacts, illusionist memorabilia, and interactive exhibits. The museum's highlight is its extensive collection of optical illusions and magic tricks that will leave you astounded. Kids and adults alike can try their hand at simple magic tricks, explore the science behind illusions, and enjoy daily magic shows in the museum's auditorium.

Tip: Make sure to check the schedule for the live magic shows and workshops. These performances offer an immersive experience into the world of magic, showcasing impressive sleight-of-hand tricks and illusions.

2. Futuroscope

Location: 24 Avenue du Téléport, 86360 Chasseneuil-du-Poitou, France

About a two-hour drive from the central Loire Valley, Futuroscope is a futuristic theme park located near Poitiers. This interactive park combines immersive technology with educational experiences, making it a fantastic day trip for families.

Futuroscope features an array of high-tech attractions, including 3D and 4D cinemas, virtual reality experiences, and interactive exhibits. Key attractions include the "Dynamic Vienne" ride, which simulates a thrilling flight over the Vienne region, and "The Time Machine," an interactive journey through the past and future.

The park also offers hands-on workshops where children can engage with science and technology in a fun and interactive way. From exploring the mysteries of space to experimenting with robotics, Futuroscope makes learning an exciting adventure.

Tip: Purchase tickets in advance and consider staying overnight in one of the park's themed hotels for a full immersive experience.

3. Musée des Beaux-Arts (Museum of Fine Arts)

Location: 3 Rue des Carmes, 37000 Tours, France

While primarily an art museum, the Musée des Beaux-Arts in Tours offers interactive and educational experiences that are perfect for families. The museum is housed in a former convent and boasts a rich collection of European paintings, sculptures, and artifacts.

The museum offers various workshops and educational programs tailored to different age groups. These interactive sessions allow visitors to engage with art in a hands-on manner, including activities like creating their own art projects inspired by the museum's collection. Kids can enjoy scavenger hunts through the galleries, which are designed to make learning about art both fun and informative.

Tip: Check the museum's schedule for family-friendly workshops and guided tours. The museum's staff often conducts interactive sessions that delve into the techniques and stories behind the artworks.

4. Le Grand Aquarium de Touraine

Location: 4 Rue du Champ de Foire, 37130 Lussault-sur-Loire, France

Le Grand Aquarium de Touraine, located near Amboise, offers a different type of interactive experience centered around marine life. This aquarium is home to a diverse collection of aquatic species from local rivers to exotic seas.

Interactive exhibits include touch pools where visitors can handle starfish and sea urchins, and digital displays that provide insights into marine biology and conservation. The aquarium also features a series of educational programs designed for children, including interactive games and storytelling sessions about marine ecosystems.

Tip: Arrive early to enjoy the interactive touch pools before they become too crowded. The aquarium also offers themed events and workshops throughout the year, so check their website for the latest information.

5. Musée de l'Imprimerie (Museum of Printing)

Location: 29 Rue du Commerce, 37000 Tours, France

For those intrigued by the art of printing and typography, the Musée de l'Imprimerie in Tours is a fascinating stop. This museum delves into the history of printing from its origins to the digital age, featuring an array of historic printing presses and typographical tools.

Interactive elements include hands-on printing workshops where visitors can create their own prints using traditional methods. The museum's educational programs are designed to engage visitors with the history of printing and its impact on communication and culture.

Tip: Participate in a workshop to get a first-hand experience of traditional printing techniques. The museum's knowledgeable staff are enthusiastic about sharing their expertise and ensuring a memorable visit.

Chapter 7: Practical Information

Getting There and Around: Transportation Tips

Getting There

By Air:

The Loire Valley does not have its own international airport, but several nearby airports serve as gateways to the region:

Tours Val de Loire Airport (TUF): Located about 7 km from the center of Tours, this small airport offers seasonal flights to and from major French cities and a few international destinations. It's a convenient option if you are heading directly to Tours. Address: Aéroport de Tours, 37210 Parçay-Meslay, France.

Nantes Atlantique Airport (NTE): Approximately 150 km west of Tours, Nantes Atlantique is a larger airport with more frequent flights from various European cities. From Nantes, you can rent a car or take a train to reach the Loire Valley. Address: Aéroport Nantes Atlantique, 44346 Bouguenais, France.

Paris Charles de Gaulle Airport (CDG): Situated about 200 km from Tours, CDG is one of the largest international airports in France. It offers extensive global connections and frequent high-speed train services (TGV) to Tours and other major cities in the Loire Valley. Address: 95700 Roissy-en-France, France.

By Train:

The train is an excellent way to reach the Loire Valley, offering comfort and scenic views. The high-speed TGV (Train à Grande Vitesse) connects major cities:

From Paris: The TGV departs from Paris Montparnasse station and arrives at Tours in just over an hour. Tickets can be purchased online through SNCF (the French national railway company) or at the station. Address: Gare Montparnasse, 75015 Paris, France.

From Nantes: Regional trains connect Nantes with Tours, with a journey time of around 2 hours. Again, tickets can be bought through SNCF or at the station. Address: Gare de Nantes, 44000 Nantes, France.

From Lyon: TGV trains from Lyon Part-Dieu station to Tours take about 3 hours. Book your tickets in advance to secure the best fares. Address: Gare de Lyon Part-Dieu, 69003 Lyon, France.

By Car:

Driving offers flexibility and allows you to explore the Loire Valley at your own pace. Major highways connect the region with Paris, Nantes, and other key cities:

From Paris: Take the A10 motorway (Autoroute du Soleil) south towards Tours. The journey is around 2 hours, depending on traffic.

From Nantes: Take the A83 motorway towards Tours. The drive takes approximately 1.5 hours.

From Lyon: Drive on the A6 motorway north, then take the A85 motorway towards Tours. Expect a drive of about 4 hours.

Car rentals are available at major airports and train stations. Opt for a GPS device or a navigation app to help with local roads and parking.

Getting Around

By Car:

Exploring the Loire Valley by car is highly recommended. The region is well-connected by a network of roads and scenic routes. Renting a car allows you to visit various châteaux and vineyards at your convenience. Popular driving routes include:

The Loire à Vélo: A dedicated cycling route that runs alongside the Loire River, offering scenic drives and access to numerous attractions.

The Château Route: A circular route connecting major châteaux such as Chambord, Chenonceau, and Amboise.

Ensure your rental car has a valid parking permit or is parked in designated areas, especially in historic towns where parking can be limited.

By Train:

The Loire Valley has an extensive regional train network that connects major towns and cities:

SNCF TER (Transport Express Régional): Regional trains provide frequent services between towns such as Tours, Blois, and Saumur. Tickets can be purchased at stations or online.

Intercités: For longer journeys within the region, Intercités trains offer comfortable services between larger cities.

By Bicycle:

Cycling is a popular and enjoyable way to explore the Loire Valley. The Loire à Vélo route offers a flat, well-signposted path that follows the Loire River, passing through vineyards, charming villages, and historical sites. Many towns, including Tours and Amboise, have bike rental services.

By Bus:

Local and regional buses provide access to smaller towns and villages not served by trains. Bus services operate from central stations in major towns such as Tours and Blois. Check schedules and routes in advance as services may be limited.

By Taxi:

Taxis and ride-sharing services are available in larger towns and cities. They offer a convenient option for short trips or if you prefer not to drive. Be sure to confirm rates and availability beforehand.

Accommodation Guide: Where to Stay for Every Budget

Luxury Stays: Indulge in Opulence

Château de Pray

Located in the heart of the Loire Valley, Château de Pray offers an unparalleled experience in a 19th-century château setting. This luxurious hotel combines historical charm with modern comfort, featuring elegantly furnished rooms with stunning views of the surrounding gardens and vineyards. The on-site restaurant provides gourmet dining, and the castle's spa offers a range of indulgent treatments.

Address: Château de Pray, 37190 Amboise, France

Website: chateaudepay.com

Les Hauts de Loire

For those who desire a truly immersive château experience, Les Hauts de Loire is a fantastic choice. Set in a vast park, this 19th-century château boasts luxurious rooms, an excellent gourmet restaurant, and a lovely outdoor pool. The property also offers bespoke activities such as wine tasting and private château tours.

Address: 12 Rue de la Paix, 41150 Onzain, France

Website: leshautsdeloire.com

Mid-Range Options: Comfort and Charm

Hôtel Le Clos d'Amboise

Situated in the heart of Amboise, Hôtel Le Clos d'Amboise is a beautifully restored 19th-century mansion. The hotel combines elegance with comfort, offering spacious rooms and a serene garden with a heated outdoor pool. It's just a short walk from the Château d'Amboise and local restaurants. The friendly staff can assist with booking local tours and activities.

Address: 27 Rue Rabelais, 37400 Amboise, France

Website: closdamboise.com

Château de Perreux

Château de Perreux, located near the charming town of Noyers-sur-Cher, provides a delightful mid-range option. This 19th-century château is surrounded by a beautiful park and offers elegant rooms, a gourmet restaurant, and a relaxing spa. It's well-positioned for exploring the nearby Château de Chenonceau and other local attractions.

Address: 16 Route de Chenonceaux, 41140 Noyers-sur-Cher, France

Website: chateaudeperreux.com

Budget-Friendly Choices: Cozy and Affordable

Hotel Ibis Blois Vallée Maillard

For travelers on a tighter budget, the Hotel Ibis Blois Vallée Maillard offers a comfortable and affordable stay. Located just outside Blois, this modern hotel features clean, functional rooms and a welcoming atmosphere. It's a great base for exploring the historic town of Blois and the surrounding châteaux without breaking the bank.

Address: 1 Avenue du Maréchal Juin, 41000 Blois, France

Website: ibis.com

Auberge de la Brenne

Situated in the village of Mézières-en-Brenne, Auberge de la Brenne offers a quaint and budget-friendly accommodation option. This charming inn features cozy rooms and a warm, rustic dining area serving local cuisine. It's a great choice for those wanting to experience rural France and explore the nearby Brenne Regional Nature Park.

Address: 14 Rue du Pont, 36290 Mézières-en-Brenne, France

Website: aubergedelabrenne.com

Unique Stays: Experience the Loire Valley Differently

Domaine de la Tortinière

For a unique experience, consider staying at Domaine de la Tortinière, a beautiful estate offering both a charming château and modern villa accommodations. Located near Tours, the property features stylish rooms, a gourmet restaurant, and an inviting pool. The estate's picturesque grounds are perfect for leisurely strolls and relaxation.

Address: 10 Route de Chissay, 37270 Montbazon, France

Website: tortiniere.com

La Maison des Vignerons

Experience life in a traditional Loire Valley vineyard at La Maison des Vignerons. This cozy guesthouse is nestled among the vineyards of Vouvray and provides an authentic taste of local wine culture. Guests can enjoy comfortable rooms, wine tastings, and access to the owners' extensive wine cellar.

Address: 6 Rue du Vau Raymond, 37210 Vouvray, France

Website: maison-des-vignerons.com

Health and Safety Tips: Staying Safe While Exploring

1. Healthcare and Emergency Services

While the Loire Valley is generally a safe destination, it's wise to familiarize yourself with local healthcare options before your trip. France has an excellent healthcare system, but knowing where to go in case of an emergency can save valuable time.

Emergency Numbers: In case of an emergency, dial 112 for ambulance services, fire department, or police. This number is valid throughout the European Union.

Hospitals and Clinics:

Centre Hospitalier Régional Universitaire de Tours: Located at 2 Boulevard Tonnellé, 37044 Tours. This is a major hospital offering comprehensive medical services.

Hôpital de Blois: Situated at 1 Avenue de Verdun, 41016 Blois. A reliable choice for medical emergencies in Blois.

Clinique Saint-Louis: Located at 14 Rue Saint-Louis, 49000 Angers. Offers specialized care and emergency services.

Pharmacies: Pharmacies in France are well-stocked and can be found easily in most towns. Look for the green cross symbol. For urgent medical advice, local pharmacists are very knowledgeable.

2. Travel Insurance

Before traveling, ensure you have adequate travel insurance. This should cover medical emergencies, trip cancellations, lost luggage, and any other unexpected events. European Health Insurance Cards (EHIC) or Global Health Insurance Cards (GHIC) can provide access to state healthcare in France, but they do not cover everything.

3. Vaccinations and Health Precautions

France is generally safe regarding health risks, but staying up-to-date with routine vaccinations is always a good idea. No specific vaccinations are required for visiting the Loire Valley, but consider the following:

Routine Vaccinations: Ensure you are up-to-date with vaccinations such as measles, mumps, rubella, and tetanus.

Tick-Borne Encephalitis: If planning to hike in forested areas, be aware of ticks, which can carry diseases. Wear long sleeves and trousers and use insect repellent.

4. Safety While Hiking and Cycling

The Loire Valley offers numerous outdoor activities, from hiking trails to cycling routes. While these activities are generally safe, taking some precautions can enhance your experience:

Hiking Trails: Follow marked trails and inform someone of your route and expected return time. Some popular trails include the Montsoreau-Méon loop and the Cormery Loop. Always carry a map and check local weather conditions before setting out.

Cycling Routes: The Loire à Vélo route is well-signposted, but always wear a helmet and be cautious of traffic, especially in urban areas. Carry a repair kit and ensure your bike is in good working order.

5. Food and Water Safety

French cuisine is renowned for its quality, but to avoid any potential issues:

Restaurants and Food: Dine at reputable restaurants and check reviews before eating out. Local markets are excellent for fresh produce, but ensure that fruits and vegetables are thoroughly washed.

Tap Water: Tap water in the Loire Valley is safe to drink. However, if you have sensitive stomachs, bottled water is widely available and can be a better option.

6. Weather and Clothing

The Loire Valley experiences a temperate climate with mild winters and warm summers. However, weather can be unpredictable:

Weather Conditions: Check the weather forecast regularly and pack accordingly. In summer, temperatures can soar, so bring sun protection, including sunscreen, a hat, and sunglasses.

Rain Gear: Rain is not uncommon, so carry a waterproof jacket or umbrella. Layers are ideal for varying temperatures throughout the day.

7. Personal Safety and Scams

While the Loire Valley is generally safe, exercising basic safety precautions is wise:

Personal Belongings: Keep your belongings secure, especially in crowded areas. Use a money belt or a secure bag.

Scams: Be cautious of common travel scams, such as overcharging or unsolicited help. Always use official services and be wary of overly friendly strangers offering assistance.

8. COVID-19 Considerations

Stay updated on any travel advisories or health regulations related to COVID-19. France may have specific entry requirements, such as proof of vaccination or negative test results. Follow local guidelines to ensure a safe trip.

Useful Contacts: Emergency Numbers and Services

Emergency Numbers

Emergency Services (Police, Fire, Ambulance): 112

Description: This is the European Union-wide emergency number. Dial 112 for immediate assistance in cases of fire, medical emergencies, or criminal activities. Operators speak English and can dispatch police, fire, or medical services as needed.

Website: European Emergency Number Association

Local Police Stations:

Tours Police Station

Address: 8 Place de la Préfecture, 37000 Tours

Phone: +33 2 47 49 72 00

Description: The main police station in Tours, this station handles general inquiries and emergencies within the city.

Blois Police Station

Address: 10 Rue des Minimes, 41000 Blois

Phone: +33 2 54 78 55 00

Description: Located in the center of Blois, this station covers local law enforcement and emergency services.

Saumur Police Station

Address: 1 Place de la Bilange, 49400 Saumur

Phone: +33 2 41 83 21 22

Description: For emergencies in Saumur, this station offers immediate police assistance.

Fire Department (Sapeurs-Pompiers): 18

Description: For fire emergencies, accidents, or rescue operations, dial 18. The fire department can respond to a wide range of emergency situations and is well-equipped for quick action.

Website: Sapeurs-Pompiers

Medical Emergencies and Ambulance Services: 15

Description: Use 15 for emergency medical assistance. This number connects you to SAMU (Service d'Aide Médicale Urgente), which provides ambulance services and urgent medical care.

Healthcare Facilities

CHRU de Tours (Tours Regional Hospital)

Address: 2 Boulevard Tonnellé, 37044 Tours

Phone: +33 2 47 47 47 47

Description: The main hospital in Tours offering comprehensive medical services, including emergency care. The hospital is well-equipped and provides specialized medical attention for various emergencies.

Hôpital de Blois (Blois Hospital)

Address: 2 Boulevard Louis Robert, 41016 Blois

Phone: +33 2 54 55 70 00

Description: Blois Hospital provides emergency medical services, surgical care, and general hospital services. The facility is equipped with emergency rooms and specialized departments.

Hôpital de Saumur (Saumur Hospital)

Address: 3 Rue de la Pinaudière, 49400 Saumur

Phone: +33 2 41 50 66 00

Description: Saumur's hospital offers emergency care, as well as general and specialized medical services. It is equipped to handle a range of medical situations.

Pharmacies

Pharmacie de la Préfecture (Tours)

Address: 5 Place de la Préfecture, 37000 Tours

Phone: +33 2 47 05 56 69

Description: This pharmacy is conveniently located near Tours' city center and offers a range of over-the-counter medications and health products.

Pharmacie Centrale (Blois)

Address: 11 Avenue de Chateauroux, 41000 Blois

Phone: +33 2 54 78 56 00

Description: A well-stocked pharmacy in Blois providing medications, health advice, and emergency supplies.

Pharmacie du Centre (Saumur)

Address: 10 Rue du Docteur Bretonneau, 49400 Saumur

Phone: +33 2 41 40 01 00

Description: Located in central Saumur, this pharmacy offers pharmaceuticals, health consultations, and emergency assistance.

Additional Contacts

Tourist Information Centers:

Tours Office de Tourisme

Address: 78 Rue Bernard Palissy, 37000 Tours

Phone: +33 2 47 64 77 00

Website: Tours Tourist Office

Blois Office de Tourisme

Address: 6 Place du Château, 41000 Blois

Phone: +33 2 54 78 40 20

Website: Blois Tourist Office

Saumur Office de Tourisme

Address: 1 Place de la Bilange, 49400 Saumur

Phone: +33 2 41 40 20 00

Website: Saumur Tourist Office

Emergency Translation Services:

Translation Service in Tours:

Address: 16 Rue Nationale, 37000 Tours

Phone: +33 2 47 66 16 16

Translation Service in Blois:

Address: 15 Rue de la Chaussée, 41000 Blois

Phone: +33 2 54 90 09 09

Conclusion

As your journey through the Loire Valley draws to a close, we hope this guide has illuminated the myriad wonders that await you in this exceptional region. From the regal splendor of its châteaux to the quaint charm of its villages, the Loire Valley offers an experience that is both captivating and deeply enriching.

You've traversed the grand halls of Château de Chambord, wandered through the lush gardens of Château de Villandry, and marveled at the elegant Château de Chenonceau. You've explored historic towns like Tours and Blois, savored the region's exquisite wines, and indulged in its culinary delights. Whether you reveled in the beauty of the Loire à Vélo cycle route or enjoyed a serene hot air balloon ride over the valley, we trust that each moment has been a cherished part of your adventure.

This guide has been crafted with the intention of providing you with not only the practical information needed to navigate the Loire Valley but also the inspiration to delve deeper into its hidden gems. As you reminisce about your journey, may the experiences and memories you've collected continue to inspire your future travels and ignite a lasting appreciation for the beauty and culture of this remarkable region.

Remember, the Loire Valley is not just a destination; it's an invitation to immerse yourself in the richness of French heritage, to explore at your own pace, and to discover the timeless allure that has captivated travelers for centuries. Whether you return to revisit your favorite châteaux, explore new corners of the region, or share the magic with loved ones, the Loire Valley will always hold a special place in your heart.

As you bid farewell to this enchanting region, may the stories of the Loire Valley continue to resonate with you, and may your travels ahead be filled with discovery, joy, and wonder. Thank you for allowing this guide to accompany you on your journey. We wish you many more adventures and a lifetime of cherished memories.

Bon voyage, and until we meet again!

Printed in Great Britain
by Amazon